We're Going on a Bar Hunt

CONSTABLE

First published in Great Britain in 2013 by Constable

11 13 15 17 19 20 18 16 14 12

Copyright in text © 2013 Josie Lloyd and Emlyn Rees
Copyright in illustrations © 2013 Gillian Johnson

The moral right of the authors is asserted

A CIP catalogue record for this book is available from the British Library.

ISBN 978-1-4721-0979-8

Page design by Design23
Printed and bound in Italy by
L.E.G.O. SpA

Constable
An imprint of
Little, Brown Book Group
Carmelite House
50 Victoria Embankment
London EC4Y 0DZ

An Hachette UK Company
www.hachette.co.uk

www.littlebrown.com

We're Going on a Bar Hunt

A Parody

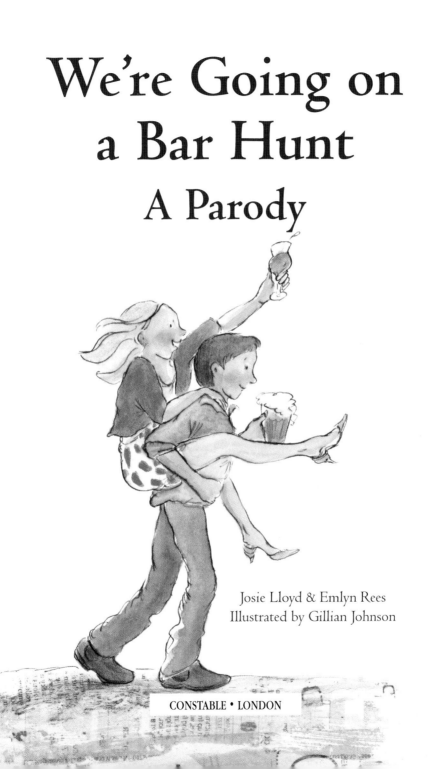

Josie Lloyd & Emlyn Rees
Illustrated by Gillian Johnson

CONSTABLE • LONDON

We're going on a bar hunt.
We're going to find a cool one.
The babysitter's booked . . .

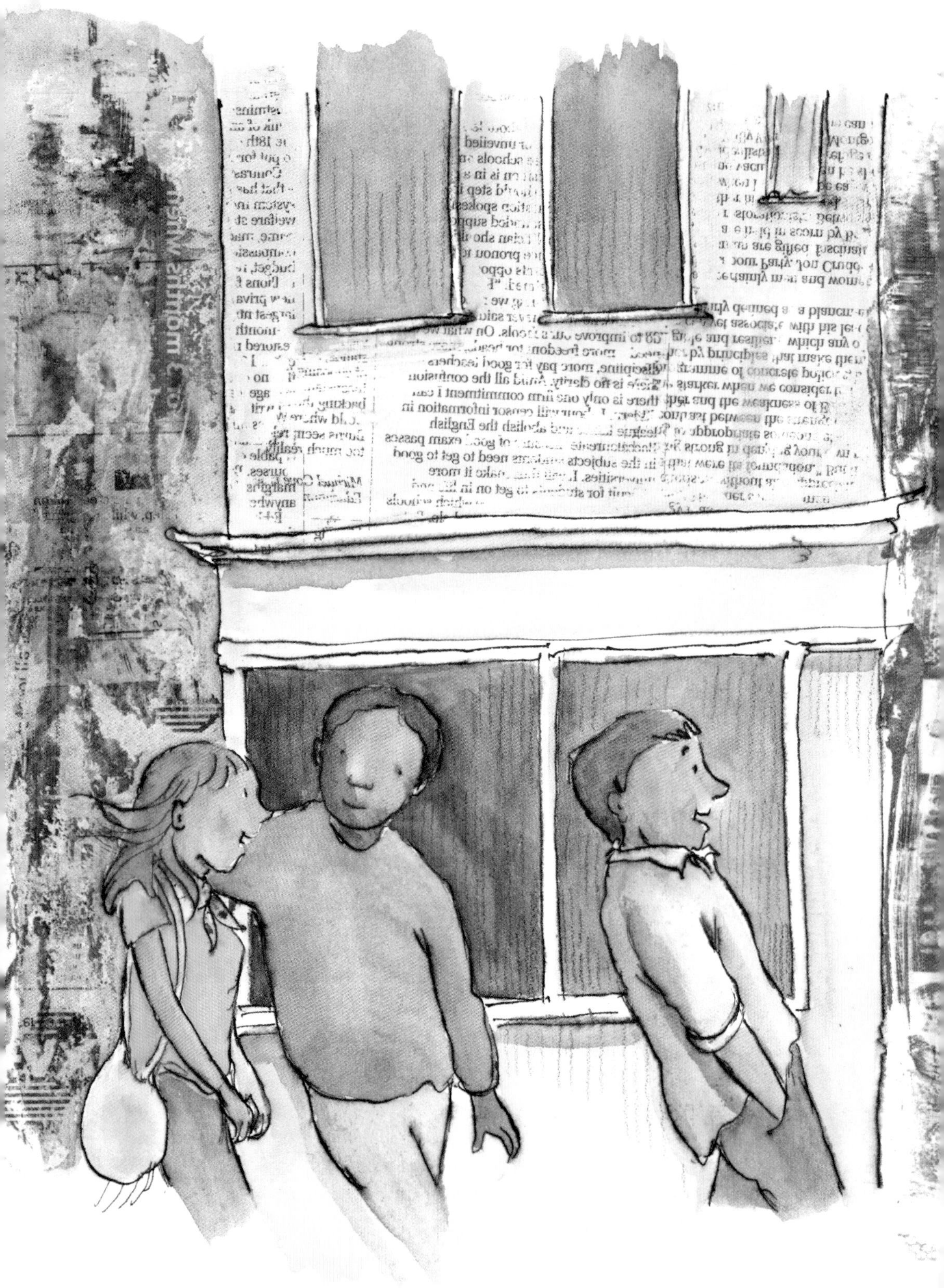

Uh-oh! An offie!
A trendy new offie!
We can't go over it.
We can't go under it.

Woo-hoo! Let's try it!

Stumble, trip!
Stumble, trip!
Stumble, trip!

We're going on a bar hunt.
We're going to find a cool one.
The babysitter's booked
We're not old!

Uh-oh! A pub!
A groovy gastro pub!
We can't go over it.
We can't go under it.
Woo-hoo! Let's try it!

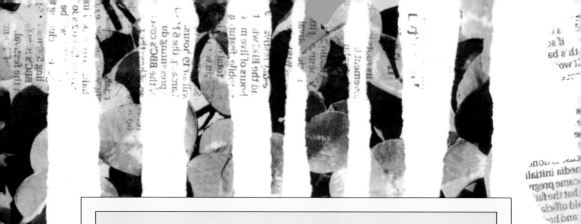

Down in one!
Down in one!
Down in one!

prospects improve. In the
looks some way off.

It is possible, of course
consumers are more pron
illusion than their banish
and that there will be a su
rising prices. But we sho
long and bitter experienc
rush is all it will be.

Water companies
Regulator must force
private monopolies to
open up, says Nils Pratle

So much for the idea that
the new head of regulato
had terrified potential bu
water companies with hi
"opaque" ownership str

done as well as provoca
re's a nagging discrepancy betw
en's late 19th-century plot and
view, and the 21st-century settin
Harrower has carefully compress
en's storyline. Once again, we
Stockmann, chief medical office
Norwegian spa, discovering tha
town's baths are toxic. Expectin
e acclaimed for his revelation,
ead Stockmann finds the whole
n turning against him; not just
oral broker, but also the liberal
ss and self-interested businessm
s trigger Stockmann's famous
frontation with the community
ich he ringingly declares that the
ority are enemies of truth and th
e minority is always right".

's always a difficult moment for
odern audience: the crusading
ormer turning into an intellectual
tocrat. But solutions can be foun
008, Greg Hicks transformed
kmann into a Nordic Coriolanus
London's Vola, and two years lat
ony Sher at the Sheffield Crucible
lied injustice had unhinged the
's wits. Here, however, nothing
ns quite right. Harrower has alter
's text so that Stockmann's
ts include not just politicians
the "gangrape of democracy", bu
whole consumer society and our
hetic selves; he reminds me of a
bom bore hanging on about the
try going to hell in a handcart.
by making the audience victims o
tmann's tirade, Jones's productio
e our passivity into endorsement.
e, Stockmann asks: "Has anyone
one good word to say about
clans?", I wondered what would
en if someone stood up, as I felt
oing, and saying, "Actually, yes."

k Fletcher is a perfectly decent
emann: pinning up wallcharts abo
eria, he's more scientific rationalis
blazing idealist, which makes the
cter's descent into ranting hysteri
er to fathom. There is lively suppo
Darrell D'Silva as the bullying
or, Niall Ashdown as a nervous
er and Charlotte Randle as a
vely sceptical Mrs Stockmann. Bu
ugh Miriam Buether has come up
an extraordinary set - all stripped
garish austerity and twinkling
- it takes more than clever design
ke this a play for today. I suspect
would have to trim Stockmann's
ric and totally rewrite Ibsen's plot
e modern world. It has, of course
ly been done with spectacular
ss in 'Jaws, which feels far closer t
's spirit than this jangling update.

el Billington
8 June. Box office: 020-7922 2923.

We're going on a bar hunt.
We're going to find a cool one.
The babysitter's booked
We're not old!

Uh-oh! A cocktail bar!
An uber funky cocktail bar.
We can't go over it.
We can't go under it.
Woo-hoo! Let's try it!

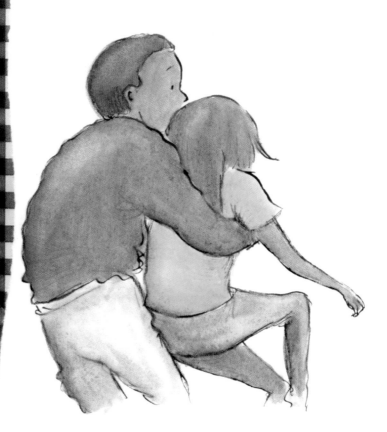

Jägerbomb! Jägerbomb! Jägerbomb!

We're going on a bar hunt.
We're going to find a cool one.
The babysitter's booked
We're not old!

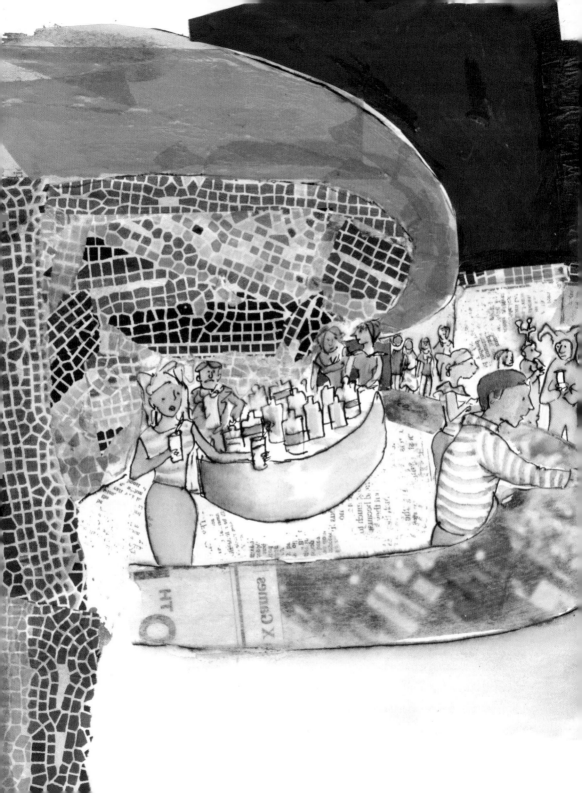

Uh-oh! A club!
A really rocking club.
We can't go over it.
We can't go under it.
Woo-hoo! Let's try it!

Conga, conga!
Conga, conga!
Conga, conga!

reduced by the bedroom tax
council tax, knowing many
Disabled people
benefits and cut services
Taxpayers Against
the 13 worst
intellectual property
to pirated DVD
We, the

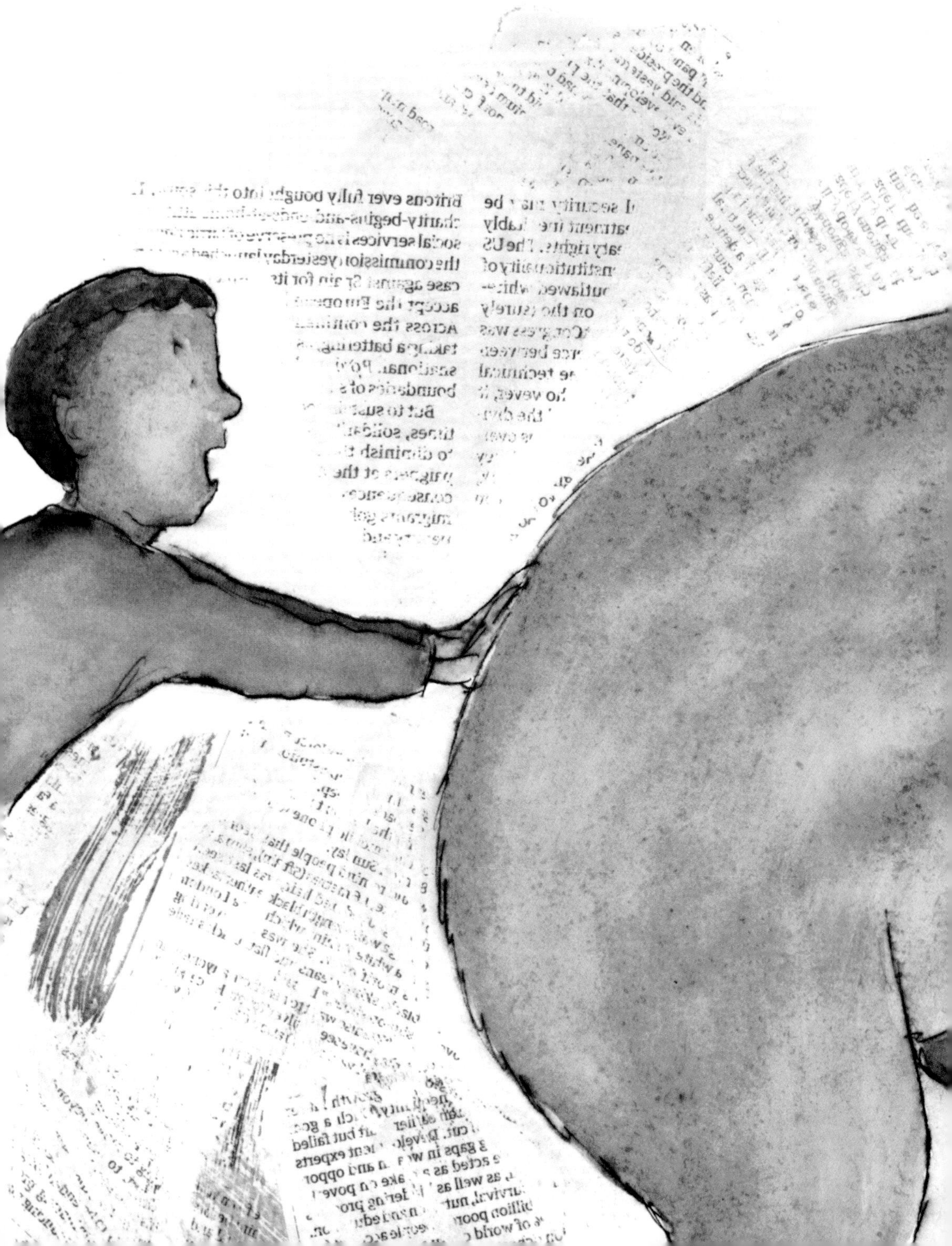

Wait! What's that?
One big blue tattoo.
Two gold shiny teeth.
Two clenched fists.

IT'S A . . . BEAR!

Quick! Back through the club!
Conga, conga! Conga, conga! Conga, conga!

Back through the cocktail bar!
Jägerbomb! Jägerbomb! Jägerbomb!

Back through the gastro pub!
Down in one! Down in one! Down in one!

Back through the offie!
Stumble trip! Stumble trip! Stumble trip!

Get to our front door. Quick! Act sober.
Oh no! We've lost Pay off the
our keys! babysitter.

Shut the front door.

Crash out on the sofa.

ROAR!
The kids are up!

ROAR!
It's 6 a.m.!

We're not going on

a bar hunt again!

Josie Lloyd and Emlyn Rees are the
bestselling authors of *Come Together*,
A Twist of Fate, *Hunted* and many
other novels. They're married and live
in Brighton with their three children.

Gillian Johnson is a prize-winning
writer and illustrator whose work has
been translated into ten languages.
She lives in Oxford with her husband
and two sons.